C·O·L·O·R·C·A·R·D·S ®

Activities
101 Ideas for
Children & Adults
Vanessa Harrison

Speechmark

DEDICATION

For Roger and Albert, and everyone in between.

ColorCards™ and ColorLibrary™ are registered trademarks of Speechmark Publishing Ltd.

First published in 2006 by
Speechmark Publishing Ltd, Telford Road, Bicester, Oxon OX26 4LQ, United Kingdom
www.speechmark.net

002-3729/Printed in Great Britain/1010

British Library Cataloguing in Publication Data

Harrison, Vanessa
    ColorCards activities
    1. Reading – Color aids
    I. Title
    372.4'12

ISBN-13: 978 086388 551 8
ISBN-10: 0 86388 551 9

Presenting an activity

Before you start

- read it through carefully
- adapt it to your precise aim and to your students' abilities
- make notes if helpful
- collect together the cards and any other material that you need

Think about

- whether you want to practise an existing skill, or teach a new one.
- the age and maturity level of your students
- their ability to attend, and to maintain concentration
- their level of understanding
- their familiarity with group activity
- whether students have physical or sensory deficits

As you go through

At the beginning of the session, make sure that the students are comfortable and can easily hear and see what you are doing. Tell them what you are about to do with them and why you are doing it.

During the session, focus on the purpose of the activity and avoid the temptation to be diverted. If you feel that the activity is not going as well as you'd hoped, change your approach, perhaps by giving more help. In this way you will achieve your teaching aim, and your students will experience success.

Pointers to successful teaching and therapy sessions

- to make an activity easier, include the following elements:
    - use few pictures and present them simply
    - choose familiar images and vocabulary
    - give instructions in a way that is easy to understand
    - provide little memory load
    - aim for a relaxed session with minimal pressure on the students
    - work away from external distractions
- make the teaching sessions lively and interesting
- know your students' names
- respond to them individually from time to time
- don't patronise them with slow or loud speech
- use simple language yourself, and don't talk too much
- consider adding gesture to help understanding
- correct in a positive way, such as modelling a right answer
- be aware of individual differences in levels of knowledge and confidence

Some of the activities in this handbook will already be familiar, and others will be new. In either case, the ideas will help you to see the huge range of possibilities for teaching and therapy with the ever-expanding ColorCards range.

Attention

Being able to attend, and to maintain concentration, are both essential for learning. Attention and concentration involve focussing on what is relevant while ignoring surrounding activity.

Attention is important both for developing language and for using it in everyday life. Socially and in more formal interaction, we need to attend so that we understand fully, and respond in the right way.

Sustaining attention is easier for students when they are fresh and relaxed, and when the topic is interesting. Make sure that the vocabulary and images that you use in the activities in this section are motivating, and familiar to the students. If some of the content is new, you will be asking them to work on understanding as well.

These activities are largely concerned with visual attention, and focus on observational skills and visual discrimination. The next section, **Listening**, involves auditory attention.

(**1**) Find it

AIM   *To focus attention*

CARDS TO USE

Use cards showing single objects.
Choose objects that your students know well.

ACTIVITY

● Show the students four or five pictures of objects, and name them together.
● While they are looking, put the pictures face down on the table.
● Ask a student to find the one you name.
● Repeat with other students, and different groups of cards.

SUITABLE SETS INCLUDE

Early Objects, Personal Items

TIP

Use more pictures to make the activity harder.

(2) Remember where

AIM   *To focus and sustain attention*

CARDS TO USE

Use cards showing single objects.
Choose objects that your students know well, and can name easily.

ACTIVITY

- Show the students three or four pictures of objects and name them together.
- Put the pictures face down in a row on the table, naming them again.
- Ask a student to name each picture in order.
- Check his answer by turning up the cards again.
- Repeat with other students and different groups of cards.

SUITABLE SETS INCLUDE

Early Objects, Personal Items

TIP

Use five or six cards to make the activity harder.

USE ALSO FOR

Sequencing

Speechmark

(3) Kim's game plus

AIM   *To focus and sustain attention*

CARDS TO USE

Use cards showing single objects.
Choose cards that your students know well, and can name easily.

ACTIVITY

- Show the students four or five pictures.
- Talk about them together.
- Add another card while the students look away.
- Show the cards to them again.
- Ask a student to find the new card.
- Repeat with other students and different groups of cards.

SUITABLE SETS INCLUDE

More Categories, Find the Link

TIP

Use more pictures to make the activity harder.
Add two pictures to a larger group.

Speechmark

(4) Kim's game

AIM   *To focus and sustain attention*

CARDS TO USE

Use cards showing single objects.
Choose objects that your students know well, and can name easily.

ACTIVITY

- Show the students five or six pictures.
- Talk about them together.
- Remove one of the cards while they look away.
- Show them the cards again.
- Ask a student to name the missing card.
- Repeat with other students and different groups of cards.

SUITABLE SETS INCLUDE

More Categories, Find the Link

TIP

Use more pictures to make the activity harder.
Remove two pictures from a larger group.

Speechmark

5 Our colour

AIM *To develop observation skills, and to sustain attention*

CARDS TO USE

Use cards showing simple images such as single objects.

ACTIVITY

- Show the students eight to twelve cards.
- Name a colour and ask a student to find all the cards with that colour in it.
- Regroup the cards and choose a different colour for the next student.

SUITABLE SETS INCLUDE

Everyday Objects, Categories

TIP

To make the activity harder, use cards with more complex images, such as activities or scenes.

To make it harder still, name a colour and ask the students to find cards *without* that colour.

(6) I spy

AIM   *To focus and sustain attention*

CARDS TO USE

Use cards showing single objects.
Choose objects that are unrelated.

ACTIVITY

- Show the students six to eight pictures and name the objects clearly.
- Give clues to one of the objects by describing where it is found. 'I spy with my little eye something that is in the bathroom.'
- Ask a student to find the right card. (He is looking for a wash bag.)
- Repeat with other students.

SUITABLE SETS INCLUDE

Possessions, More Categories

TIP

To make the activity harder, use more cards and choose objects that are more closely related.

USE ALSO FOR

Understanding
Classification

Speechmark

(7) Hunt the object

AIM *To sustain attention*

CARDS TO USE

Use small cards showing objects.
Choose pictures that match objects in the room.
You can use existing objects, or hide a selection of small items before the session.

ACTIVITY

- Give each student two or three pictures.
- Name the objects, and make sure the students are familiar with them.
- Ask them to look round the room and find the objects on their cards.
- Let them bring their objects back to the table.

Examples of objects to match with pictures (these pictures are from *Categories*)

apple	carrot	lunchbox
bag	cup	pencil case
ball	spoon	screwdriver
shoe	baseball cap	hammer
hairbrush	toothbrush	jigsaw puzzle

TIP

To make the activity harder, ask them to leave the pictures behind as they look for their objects.

USE ALSO FOR

Auditory memory
Understanding

(8) Homing in

AIM   *To sustain attention*

CARDS TO USE

Use cards showing a scene or event.

ACTIVITY

- Display six to eight cards on the table, or on the walls of the room.
- Tell the students that they are going to find pictures that you describe. They will have to listen carefully to hear all the information.
- Describe an activity from one of the pictures, gradually adding more detail. 'It's a girl… she is wearing something red… she is sitting down… she is drinking.'
- Ask a student to find the right picture.
- Continue with other students, and descriptions of different pictures.

SUITABLE SETS INCLUDE

Single cards from *Sequencing* sets, *Personal Safety, Social Behaviour*

USE ALSO FOR

Listening
Understanding

Listening

istening is more than the simple act of hearing. It is an active skill that is concerned with making sense of what is heard. It is the basis of learning language.

As you encourage careful listening, make sure that the students are sitting comfortably, and that they are not likely to be distracted by nearby activity or noise. They will find it easier to listen if they look at who is speaking. The students will settle better and be more relaxed if they speaker uses a quiet voice when they speak. Don't expect them to be able to listen intently for too long. This is especially important if your students are young or immature.

The activities in this section start with recognising sounds in the environment. Later activities involve listening to words, then to phrases, and finally to complex speech with a range of content words and grammatical forms.

9 What's that sound?

AIM *To recognise home sounds*

CARDS TO USE

Collect together some familiar objects that make distinctive sounds. Find pictures to match them.

ACTIVITY

- Show the objects to the students and talk about them together.
- Demonstrate the sound that each object makes.
- Let the students have a turn with objects that are safe to handle.
- Put the pictures on the table, and remove the sound makers.
- Out of sight of the students, activate one of the objects and ask a student to match the sound to its picture.
- Continue with the other sounds.

Examples of sound makers to match with pictures (these pictures are from *Home*)

radio	can opener
hand whisk	dustpan and brush
electric kettle	matches
scissors	stapler
wooden spoon (and bowl)	electric fan
vegetable peeler (and potato)	knife (and vegetable)

TIP

To make the activity harder, choose a new group of sounds and play them without demonstrating them first. If you make your own human sounds, you won't need to collect objects.

Examples of sounds to match with pictures (these pictures are from *Indoor Sounds*)

coughing	laughing
whistling	yawning
clapping	snoring
sneezing	crying

USE ALSO FOR

Auditory memory

Speechmark

(10) Sounds around

AIM   *To recognise environmental sounds*

CARDS TO USE

Use cards and the accompanying CD from *Indoor Sounds*.

ACTIVITY

- Show the students one group of ten pictures from *Indoor Sounds*, such as Having Fun.
- Talk about the pictures together and play the sounds that the people or objects make. Link each sound with its sound maker.
- Share the pictures among the students, and tell them that they must listen carefully. When they hear a sound that matches one of their pictures, they must hold it up.
- Play the sounds on the CD in random order. Check that the students match the right picture to each sound.

TIP

To make the activity harder, use pictures and sounds from *Outdoor Sounds*. These are mainly less familiar.

USE ALSO FOR

Auditory memory

(11) Sound sequencing

AIM   *To recognise two environmental sounds and to remember them both*

CARDS TO USE

Use cards and the CD from any of the *Listening Skills* packs.

ACTIVITY

- Show the students six pictures from one of the packs. Choose items that make sounds very different from each other.
- Play the sounds from the CD, and for each one ask a student to match it to its picture.
- Explain that you are going to play two of the sounds again, but this time they must wait until they have heard them both before they match them to the cards.
- Play two sounds, and ask a student to find both pictures

TIP

The activity is harder if the students have to find the cards in the order that you played them.

It is also harder if you use more cards and ask them to remember three sounds.

USE ALSO FOR

Auditory memory

(12) Kim's sound game

AIM   *To encourage careful listening*

CARDS TO USE

Use cards and the matching CD from *Indoor Sounds* or *Outdoor Sounds*

ACTIVITY

- Show three or four pictures of sound-makers to the students, and talk about them together.
- Play the sounds they make, and ask the students to match them to their pictures.
- Remove the pictures. Play all the sounds except one again.
- Ask a student to name the missing sound.

TIP

Use more sounds to make the activity harder.

USE ALSO FOR

Auditory memory

(13) What else?

AIM   *To encourage careful listening*

CARDS TO USE

Use cards showing several objects, or cards showing a scene.

ACTIVITY

- Show the students one of the pictures.
- Ask them to take turns to name something in the picture.
- Anyone who repeats an item is 'out' for the rest of that round.
- Continue with different pictures.

SUITABLE SETS INCLUDE

What's Inside? What's Different? What's Missing?

TIP

Encourage the students to look for tiny objects or parts of larger things to make a longer list.

USE ALSO FOR

Attention

Auditory memory

14 Chinese whispers

AIM   *To encourage careful listening*

CARDS TO USE

Use cards showing objects.

Play a version of this well-known game using picture cards as visual prompts.

ACTIVITY

- Put six to eight cards on the table and whisper the name of one of them to the first student.
- Ask him to whisper the name to the next student, and so on round the circle.
- The final student points to the picture he thinks is being described.
- Continue with other cards.

SUITABLE SETS INCLUDE

Everyday Objects, Animals & Birds

TIP

For a harder activity, whisper a description of the picture to the first student, so that there is more to listen to, and more to pass on.

USE ALSO FOR

Auditory memory

(15) Beat the word

AIM   To listen for the number of syllables in words

CARDS TO USE
Use cards showing single objects, or cards showing actions.
Choose a group of images to illustrate different numbers of syllables.

ACTIVITY
- Show the students three pictures with different numbers of syllables. You might choose 'bus', 'lorry' and 'caravan'.
- Say each word clearly, clapping the syllables as you speak.
- Let the students copy you.
- Introduce new groups of pictures.
- Start off with the group clapping the syllables, and move on to individual students as they become more confident.

Examples of words with one to three syllables:
(these pictures are from *Find the Link*)

One	Two	Three
cow	rabbit	butterfly
sheep	donkey	crocodile
horse	goldfish	elephant
pig	camel	kangaroo
car	glider	monorail
train	tractor	motor bike
yacht	digger	submarine
tram	rocket	aeroplane

USE ALSO FOR
Attention

© Vanessa Harrison 2006

16 Sound link

AIM   *To link words to their initial sounds*

CARDS TO USE

Use cards showing single objects.
Choose objects that have four to six different initial sounds.
You might have two or three cards for each sound.

ACTIVITY

- Go through the pictures and name them clearly.
- Say one of the initial sounds.
- Ask a student to find an image to match it.
- Repeat for the other pictures.
- Now pick up a picture and name it again.
- Ask a student to tell you the sound it begins with.
- Repeat for the other pictures.

SUITABLE SETS INCLUDE

Categories, More Categories

TIP

Start with a group of sounds that are very different from each other, such as 'm', 's' and 'k'.
Move on to more similar sounds, such as 'b', 'd' and 'g', when the students are ready.
A harder activity is to ask the students to think of other objects that begin with the sounds that you are using.

USE ALSO FOR

Attention

17 Rhyming pairs

AIM   *To develop rhyming skills*

CARDS TO USE

Use cards showing single objects.
Choose objects with names of one or two syllables, and that rhyme with other familiar objects.

ACTIVITY

- Put five or six pictures on the table.
- Say the names of the objects clearly.
- Say a word that rhymes with one of the objects. 'Rake.'
- Ask a student to find the right picture. (He is looking for a cake.)

TIP

Start with words that have endings very different from each other. Progress to words that sound more similar and are harder to distinguish.

Example of starter word list (these pictures are from *Categories*)
Pictures – bag, grass, train, hat, tree, bike
Rhyming words – rag, pass, lane, cat, flea, like

Example of harder word list (these pictures are from *Categories*)
Pictures – plane, snail, drill, owl, cow, ball
Rhyming words – rain, pale, hill, towel, now, fall

ColorCards Activities © Vanessa Harrison 2006

Understanding

It is easy to overlook the importance of understanding as part of language. The emphasis is naturally on speaking. In many situations, understanding is helped by context and by other clues. Students with immature understanding may rely partly on following others to understand what they need to know.

Understanding is central to learning and to using language. To take meaning from spoken language, students need to understand word sense and word relationships. They must be able to follow instructions and explanations. They must understand questions. They need to be able to follow stories and to take part in conversations. They also need to be able to work out the central meaning of what is said, make inferences, understand the subtleties of language and look beyond the literal meaning.

The activities in this section will give you ideas of how to work on the aspects of understanding that you need for your students.

(18) Object picture match

AIM *To understand that pictures can represent objects*

CARDS TO USE

Use cards showing objects.
Choose vocabulary that the students know well.
Find objects to match the pictures.
You will need six to eight sets of pictures and objects.

ACTIVITY

- Give the objects one at a time to the students, name them, and let them handle them.
- Then put them all down on the table.
- Show the students one of the pictures.
- Ask a student to put the picture with its matching object.
- Continue with other students, and different pictures.

Examples of objects to match with pictures (these pictures are from *Early Objects*)

ball	teddy	soap
car	banana	clock
flower	toothbrush	comb

TIP

If a student can't find the right object, name the picture as you show it to him.
The activity is easier if the pictures match the objects closely.

19 Action!

AIM   *To understand that pictures can represent actions*

CARDS TO USE

Use cards showing actions.

Choose vocabulary that the students know well.

You will need six to eight pictures.

ACTIVITY

- Show the cards to the students and name what the people are doing.
- Say that you are going to do one of the actions. 'I'm going to walk.'
- As you carry out the action ask a student to find the picture that matches it.
- Then let him join in.

Examples of actions to match with pictures (these pictures are from *Basic Verbs*)

sleeping	smiling	sneezing
walking	pointing	yawning
crying	dancing	jumping

TIP

A harder activity is to use actions that have an object. In this case, mime the activities.

Examples of actions with objects to match with pictures (these pictures are from *Familiar Verbs*)

cleaning boots	grating cheese	mixing a cake
pouring juice	smelling flowers	spreading butter
stroking a dog	watering plants	blowing bubbles

(20) What's it for?

AIM   *To understand objects from their function*

CARDS TO USE

Use cards showing single objects.

Choose objects with different functions.

ACTIVITY

- Put five or six pictures on the table.
- Talk about them with the students.
- Describe one of the objects by its function: 'It's something you write with'.
- Ask a student to find the right picture.
- Repeat with other pictures, and then introduce a different group of cards.

SUITABLE SETS INCLUDE

Home, Personal Items

TIP

To make the activity easier, mime the action as you speak.

USE ALSO FOR

Classification

(21) What's it like?

This page may be photocopied for instructional use only *ColorCards Activities* © Vanessa Harrison 2006

AIM   *To develop understanding of adjectives*

CARDS TO USE

Use cards showing pictures of single objects.

Choose pictures with different attributes.

ACTIVITY

- Put five or six pictures on the table.
- Name them with the students.
- Ask a student to find something that is 'long' or something that is 'cold'.
- Continue with the other pictures, using a different adjective each time.
- Repeat with another group of pictures.

TIP

To make the activity harder, choose pictures showing objects that have some similarities, and use two adjectives to describe them.

Examples of objects to describe with two adjectives (these pictures are from *Find the Link*)

orange	banana	carrot
grapes	mushroom	yoghurt
cake	apple	ice cream

USE ALSO FOR

Classification

22 Where it is

AIM   *To develop understanding of prepositions*

CARDS TO USE

Use cards showing scenes.
Choose seven or eight pictures.

ACTIVITY

- Show a picture to the students.
- Ask a student to find an object or a person in the picture by describing its position. 'It's under the table.'
- Continue with other items in the same picture, and then move on to another scene.

TIP

The activity is harder if the scene is busy. In this case, use two prepositions to pinpoint items. 'It's on the tray, next to the biscuits.'

SUITABLE SETS INCLUDE

For one preposition – *Adjectives, Prepositions*
For two prepositions – *What's Different? What's Inside?*

Speechmark P

(23) Listen and look

AIM To find objects by description

CARDS TO USE

Use cards showing single objects.
Choose pictures showing small everyday items. These should be well known to the students.

ACTIVITY

- Put ten to twelve cards in different parts of the room. They should be easy to find.
- Tell the students that they are going to find some pictures of objects. They will have to work out what they are from the descriptions.
- Ask a student to find 'a little plastic object with numbers on, that is useful for doing sums'. (He is looking for a calculator.)
- Ask another to find 'a rectangular leather object that you need when you go shopping'. (He is looking for a wallet.)
- Let the other students decide whether the finder returns with the right object.

Examples of pictures to hide (these pictures are from *Possessions*)

calculator	wallet
key ring	guitar
sunglasses	measuring tape
purse	binoculars
watch	playing cards
mirror	hairdryer

USE ALSO FOR

Auditory memory
Classificiation

(24) Not again

AIM *To develop understanding of negatives*

CARDS TO USE

Use cards showing opposite attributes. These can be on a single card or on paired cards.

Choose seven or eight paired objects that are well known to the students.

ACTIVITY

- Show them the pairs and talk about them together.
- Introduce the word 'not' with the adjectives. 'This bag is big; this bag is not big.'
- Show another pair of objects, and ask a student to show you the one that is 'new' and the one that is 'not new'.
- Continue with other students and different cards.

SUITABLE SETS INCLUDE

Adjectives, Early Opposites

(25) After the party

AIM *To make associations*

CARDS TO USE

Use cards showing single objects.

Choose objects that could belong to specific people.

You will also need a list of these people.

ACTIVITY

- Explain to the students that they will be clearing up after a party. The guests left in a hurry and everyone left something behind. They will have to try to match these possessions with the right owners, so that they can return them.
- Put eight to ten pictures face up on the table.
- Talk through the objects with the students.
- Read out the first name on your list.
- Ask a student to find what he or she left behind.
- Continue with the other people on your list.

Examples of objects to link with people (these pictures are from *Possessions*)

hairdryer for a hairdresser

binoculars for a bird watcher

guitar for a musician

stacking cups for a baby

briefcase for an office worker

backpack for a hiker

suitcase for a traveller

lunchbox for a schoolgirl

road map for a driver

oil paints for an artist

USE ALSO FOR

Classification

Life skills

Speechmark

26 Clue by clue

AIM　*To build up the identity of an object from a series of clues*

CARDS TO USE

Use cards showing simple objects.
Choose objects that your students know well.

ACTIVITY

● You are going to give a series of clues so that the students can guess an object. Start with general information and move on to specific points.
● Choose a card and give a clue about it to a student. 'It's made of metal.'
● Give the same clue and a new one to the next student. 'It's made of metal, and it's big.'
● Add a clue for the next student. 'It's made of metal, it's big, and it takes you from place to place.'
● Give the next student the final clue. 'It's made of metal, it's big, it takes you from place to place and it has two wheels.' He is looking for a bicycle.
● Continue with other students and different pictures.

SUITABLE SETS INCLUDE

Home, Possessions

USE ALSO FOR

Classification

(27) Phone call

AIM   *To make inferences*

CARDS TO USE

Use cards showing single objects.

Choose pictures of household items.

ACTIVITY

- Explain to the students that they are going to listen to someone talking on the phone. She has been shopping, and is telling her friend about what she has bought. She won't be saying the names of the things, so they will have to listen carefully to see if they can work out what they are.
- Put eight to ten cards face up on the table, and tell the students that these are the things that the woman bought.
- Pretend to be talking on the phone, and refer to one of the items. 'I'll put it on the kitchen worktop, and use it at breakfast time.' (He is looking for a toaster.)
- Ask a student to find the right picture.
- If needed, give a further clue. 'I usually buy sliced bread, so it will be easy to use.'

Examples of objects to talk about (these pictures are from *Home*)

toaster	kitchen bin
dining table	bookcase
cushions	first aid kit
dining chair	clock
bathroom scales	fridge

USE ALSO FOR

Life skills

(28) Name the story

AIM   *To understand the main theme of a story*

CARDS TO USE

Use whole sequences.

Choose sequences that tell a story.

ACTIVITY

- Go through a sequence with the students, telling them the story.
- When you have finished, ask a student what the story is about.
- Tell the students that you need a name for this story.
- Ask them for their ideas.
- Encourage them to think of a short, snappy title rather than an overall description of the sequence.

SUITABLE SETS INCLUDE

Sequences: 4-Step, Sequences: 6 & 8-Step for Children, Sequences: 6 & 8-Step for Adults

TIP

To make the activity easier, give them a choice of titles to choose from.

(29) Think again

ColorCards Activities © Vanessa Harrison 2006. This page may be photocopied for instructional use only.

AIM   To understand sentences with two contrasting ideas

CARDS TO USE

Use small cards showing objects.
Choose objects that you can describe with a riddle.

ACTIVITY

- Put eight to ten cards face up on the table.
- Tell the students that you are going to ask them to find an object by listening to a clue. They will have to work out which one you mean.
- Give a clue in the form of a riddle to a student. 'It has a house but no window.'
- Help him if necessary to find a picture of a snail.
- Continue with the other students and different riddles.

Examples of pictures and riddles

(these pictures are from *Early Objects*)

Radio	It talks but doesn't have a mouth.
TV	It's grey, but you usually see it in colour.
Clock	It has hands, but no fingers.
Swing	It takes you for a ride, but you don't go anywhere.
Butterfly	It has wings, but it isn't a bird.
Tree	It has a bark, but doesn't make a noise.
Ice cream	It's good to eat, but disappears if you're not quick.
Dog	He's your best friend, but doesn't wear clothes.
Ball	It can fly through the air, but doesn't have wings.
Sand pit	You can dig in this, but not grow flowers.

(these pictures are from *Categories*)

Guitar	It has a head and a neck, but isn't a person.
Keyboard	It has keys, but can't open a door.
Sheep	It has a warm coat, but didn't buy it in a shop.
Parrot	It talks, but can't understand what you say.
Cauliflower	It has a head, but no eyes.
Plane	It can fly, but doesn't flap its wings.
Gift	It's something very nice, but we don't know what.
Owl	It is wise, but can't talk to you.
Saw	It has teeth, but doesn't bite.

30 Who can it be?

This page may be photocopied for instructional use only. ColorCards Activities © Vanessa Harrison 2006

AIM To understand idioms and non-literal language

CARDS TO USE
Use cards showing single actions.

ACTIVITY
- Put eight to ten cards face-up on the table.
- Tell the students that you are going to ask them, in turn, to find a person. They have to work out who it is.
- Describe a picture to a student, using an idiom. 'He's making his voice heard.'
- Help him, if necessary, to find the picture of a crying baby.
- Continue with the other students and different idioms.

Examples of pictures and idioms
(these pictures are from *Basic Verbs*)

Eating a banana	He's grabbing a bite.
Riding a bike	He's going for a spin.
Opening a biscuit box	He's feeling peckish.
Writing a letter	He's making a note.
Dancing	She wants to be a star.
Carrying toys	He's got his hands full.
Walking	She's going for a stroll.
Jumping	He's full of beans.
Watching TV	He'll get square eyes.
Sleeping	He needs to hit the sack.

(these pictures are from *Familiar Verbs*)

Biting Chocolate	She's having a snack.
Laying the table	He's thinking it's all work and no play.
Listening to music	She's in a world of her own.
Typing	She's getting down to it.
Spilling soup	She's getting in a mess.
Watering plants	She's got green fingers.
Tripping	She's going to be head over tail.
Trying on a jacket	She wants to look good.
Helping the woman	She's giving a helping hand.
Blowing bubbles	He's having a fun time.

Auditory Memory

We have to be able to hold on to auditory information for long enough to respond in the right way. This is particularly important when we are listening to directions, explanations or instructions.

In the activities in this section, make sure that you use familiar vocabulary and that the students understand fully what you say. Choose materials and topics that are interesting to them. Reduce distractions as far as possible and increase the memory load gradually.

In the early stages, let the students see pictures of items that they need to remember so that they are helped by visual memory. Later, let them rely on auditory memory alone. To help students who find these activities difficult, try suggesting strategies to help memory. Picturing objects in their heads, or thinking of their initial sounds or letters can be helpful.

(31) Say it again

AIM   *To remember word order*

CARDS TO USE

Use cards showing objects, or cards showing actions.
Choose vocabulary that the students know well.

ACTIVITY

- Show the students six to eight pictures and name them.
- Remove the pictures from view.
- Say the names of two of the pictures.
- Ask a student to repeat the names, in the right order.
- Show him the cards to check his answer.
- Repeat with other students.

SUITABLE SETS INCLUDE

Basic Verbs, Leisure Time

TIP

To make this activity harder, use a larger group of pictures and name three of them.

USE ALSO FOR

Listening
Sequencing

(32) This and that

AIM   *To remember two separate items*

CARDS TO USE

Use cards showing objects.
Choose vocabulary that the students know well.

ACTIVITY

- Keep the cards hidden from the students.
- Look at the first card and say, 'on this card, I can see a hammer.' Look at the next card and say, 'and on this card, I can see a yoghurt.'
- Choose a student, and ask him what you saw on the two cards.
- Show him the cards to check his answer.
- Continue in this way, so that the student has to remember two separate objects each time.

TIP

For a harder activity, use actions instead of objects.
Name three separate items if everyone is coping well.

SUITABLE SETS INCLUDE

For objects – *Everyday Objects, Transport & Vehicles, Animals & Birds*
For actions – any *Verb* set

USE ALSO FOR

Attention

(33) Describe it

AIM   *To remember concept words*

CARDS TO USE

Use cards showing single objects.
Choose vocabulary that the students know well.

ACTIVITY

- Keep the cards hidden from the students.
- Tell them that you are going to talk about some objects, and that they should try to imagine what they are like.
- Look at a card and describe the object using two adjectives, 'a big, red ball' or 'short, striped socks'.
- Ask a student to tell you about what is on the card. If he just names the object, ask him to tell you more about it.
- Show him the card to check his answer.

SUITABLE SETS INCLUDE

Everyday Objects, Categories, More Categories

TIP

The activity is harder if you ask the students to recall three concept words, 'a big, soft, blue bag' or 'a little, silver, round watch'.

USE ALSO FOR

Classification
Expression

(34) Instructions

AIM   *To remember instructions of increasing length*

CARDS TO USE

Use small cards showing single objects.
Choose vocabulary that the students know well.
You will also need two toy animals.

ACTIVITY

- Choose a chair for the student having a turn. Put five or six pictures and the two toys on the table so that they are easy to see and to reach.
- Tell the students that you are going to ask them to give pictures to the toys, but that they must wait until you have finished speaking before they start.
- Ask the first student to 'give the keys to the rabbit'. He has to remember 'keys' and 'rabbit'.
- Continue with the other students.
- When the students are ready, ask them to remember three words. 'Give the frog and the torch to the bear.' They have to remember 'frog', 'torch' and 'bear'.
- You can ask them to remember four words by using both animals. 'Give the candle to the bear, and give the gloves to the rabbit.' They have to remember 'candle', 'bear', 'gloves' and 'rabbit'.

SUITABLE SETS INCLUDE

Categories, More Categories, Find the Link

TIP

For older students, replace the toys with small boxes of different colours or shape, and say 'Put the cake in the yellow box', or 'Put the cat and the snake in the green box.'

USE ALSO FOR

Understanding

(35) Getting warmer

AIM *To remember instructions*

CARDS TO USE

Use small cards showing single objects.
You will need a card for each student.

ACTIVITY

- While the students are not looking, hide some pictures round the room.
- Tell a student to find the picture 'under the table'.
- Tell another to find the picture 'on the window sill'.
- Continue with the other students.
- Ask them to bring back their pictures, and to name them.
- While they are not looking, hide the pictures again, but this time, make them harder to find.
- Then give a longer instruction to each student. Use phrases such as 'under the red box on the shelf', or 'inside the green book on the desk'.

SUITABLE SETS INCLUDE

More Categories, Find the Link

TIP

Hide pictures for up to four students only at a time.

USE ALSO FOR

Attention
Understanding

(36) I went to market

AIM   *To improve auditory memory*

CARDS TO USE

Use cards showing objects.
Choose pictures of objects that the students might like to buy.

ACTIVITY

- Sit in a circle and give every student two or three pictures, which they must keep hidden from the others. Make sure that you have some pictures too.
- Look at your first card, and say: 'I went to market and bought a lemon'.
- The student next to you has to look at his first card and then say 'I went to market and bought a lemon and a pair of gloves'.
- Continue round the circle until everyone has had a turn, or there are too many things to remember.

SUITABLE SETS INCLUDE

Possessions, Personal Items

TIP

Allow the odd clue or peep at a card to keep the activity flowing, and to encourage success.

USE ALSO FOR

Attention
Turn-taking

(37) One in three

AIM   *To remember one of three items*

CARDS TO USE

Use cards showing several small objects.
Choose vocabulary that the students know well.

ACTIVITY

- Keep the cards hidden from the students.
- Look at the first card, and say 'a bike, a car and a watering can'.
- Choose a student, and ask 'a bike, a car and what else?'
- Show him the picture to check his answer.
- Continue with different pictures for the other students.

SUITABLE SETS INCLUDE

What's Inside? What's Different? Odd One Out

TIP

The activity is harder if you ask the students to recall the first or the second item. 'A bike, a watering can, and what was in the middle?' or 'A car and a watering can; what came first?'

USE ALSO FOR

Listening

Sequencing

Sequencing is important in a number of ways. Some sequencing takes place in space. The order of words on a page is a good example. Other sequencing takes place in time, such as the order of words in spoken language.

Sequencing skills are also important to understand time. The knowledge that daily activities happen in a predictable order is followed by the understanding of time itself. Use words relating to time as you do these activities. Talk about parts of the day such as lunchtime and break-time. Mention actual times too when working with the sequencing sets.

As you work with activities in this section, remember to ask the students to sequence the pictures from left to right. This will reinforce the skill needed in reading and writing.

These activities deal with the concepts of order and time. Some activities also give you the opportunity to ask the students to describe and explain events.

(38) Getting bigger

AIM   *To sequence objects by size*

CARDS TO USE

Use cards showing single objects.
Choose pictures of objects that have different sizes.

ACTIVITY

- Show the students four or five pictures of objects.
- Ask them to put the objects in a row, in the size order that they would be in real life.
- Help them to put the smallest object on the left so that the largest is on the right.
- Repeat with another group of cards.

Example of a suitable list of objects (these pictures are from *Categories*)

grapes
hairbrush
school bag
guitar
deck chair

(39) Sequencing activities

AIM *To understand order*

CARDS TO USE

Use whole sequences from a *Sequencing* set.
Choose sequences that clearly show the progress of an activity.

ACTIVITY

- Put the cards of one sequence randomly face up on the table.
- Describe the first part of the activity.
- Ask a student to find the corresponding card and to put it down.
- Describe the second part of the activity.
- Ask a student to find the right card as before.
- Continue with other students and the rest of the cards in that sequence, making sure that they sequence from left to right.

TIP

The activity is harder if you describe the whole sequence before the students put the cards down.

40 Spot the mistake

AIM
To understand order

CARDS TO USE
Use whole sequences from a *Sequencing* set.
Choose sequences of a suitable length for your students.

ACTIVITY
- Lay out a sequence in front of the students with one of the cards in the wrong place.
- Ask a student to go through the sequence to find the mistake.
- Ask him to order the sequence correctly.
- Continue with other students and different sequences.

TIP
Sequences telling a story are generally harder than those showing an everyday activity.

Speechmark

(41) The right place

AIM *To understand order*

CARDS TO USE

Use whole sequences from a *Sequencing* set.
Choose sequences of a suitable length for your students.

ACTIVITY

- Go through a sequence with the students and help them to put the cards into the correct order.
- While they look away, remove one card and close the gap.
- Give this card to a student, and ask him to put it back in the right place.
- Talk through the story again with him to check his answer
- Continue with other students, removing different cards.
- Change to new sequences from time to time.

(42) Line up

AIM *To understand order, and to work together*

CARDS TO USE

Use whole sequences from a *Sequencing* set.

You will need to match the number of cards in the sequence to the number of students taking part. (The sequence lengths in ColorCards *Sequencing* sets vary from two to eight cards.)

ACTIVITY

- Choose a sequence.
- Put it down in front of the students, and go through the activity or story with them.
- Ask one of the students to be the leader.
- Give them the cards randomly, and ask them to sort themselves into the order of the sequence. Let the leader help the others as needed.
- Ask them in turn to describe their own part of the sequence.

TIP

Sequences telling a story are generally harder than those describing an everyday activity.

Start off with up to four students and a four-part sequence. It is a harder activity with six or eight students.

USE ALSO FOR

Turn-taking

Life skills

(43) Continuing stories

AIM *To improve sequencing and logical thought*

CARDS TO USE

Use cards showing objects, people and animals.
Choose a variety of images that your students will easily understand.

ACTIVITY

- Give the students one picture each, and keep one for yourself.
- Start off a story using your picture. 'This little boy wasn't feeling very well, so his mother…'
- Ask the first student to continue the story, using his picture. '…gave him some juice and…'
- Ask the second student to continue. '…found his teddy.'
- Continue round the group so that everyone includes his picture. Be prepared to help when a picture doesn't fit in easily.

SUITABLE SETS INCLUDE

Categories, Early Objects, How's Teddy?

USE ALSO FOR

Turn-taking
Using language

44 ABC

AIM *To sequence words in alphabetical order*

CARDS TO USE

Use cards showing simple objects.
Choose objects whose names begin with different letters.

ACTIVITY

- Put about four cards face-up on the table.
- Name the objects with the students.
- Talk together about their initial letters.
- Ask a student to sequence them in alphabetical order.
- Be prepared to go through the alphabet with him if he needs help.
- Continue with other students and different cards.

SUITABLE SETS INCLUDE

Find the Link, Categories

TIP

Change the number of cards you use to fit in with the students' abilities.
To make the activity more difficult, include some words that start with the same letter.

USE ALSO FOR

Auditory memory

Speechmark

Turn-taking

Turn-taking is part of social interaction, and is an important element in learning and work situations. Students need to learn to wait for their turn, and to be ready when it comes. Turn-taking involves being able to listen, to maintain attention, follow the flow and to respond appropriately.

All the activities in this book involve some turn-taking, but the activities in this section specifically focus on it. In some activities, the students take turns in a predictable order. In others, they have to judge when to take an active part.

Remember to make opportunities for people who are more reluctant to join in.

As you use activities in this section, help the students to make their contributions relevant, timely and of a suitable length. In a group activity, all members should be able to wait and listen for most of the time.

(45) Mystery envelopes

AIM *To take turns in a group activity*

CARDS TO USE

Use cards showing objects or cards showing actions.
Choose three pictures for each student.
You will also need some envelopes.

ACTIVITY

- Give each student a 'mystery envelope' with three pictures inside.
- In turn, ask them to take a picture out of their envelope, and to name the object or the action.
- Repeat the activity until the students have named all three of their pictures.

SUITABLE SETS INCLUDE

How Many? Early Actions, More Categories

TIP

For a harder activity, use cards showing scenes, and ask the students to describe what is happening.

USE ALSO FOR

Sequencing

(46) Pass the picture

AIM   *To wait, and then take a turn*

CARDS TO USE

Use cards showing single objects, or cards showing simple actions. You will also need a radio, a CD player, or an instrument to play.

ACTIVITY

- Seat the students in a circle and give one of them a picture.
- Play some music while they pass the picture around the circle.
- When you stop the music, the student holding the card has either to name it, or say something about it.
- Change the picture, and continue with the activity.

SUITABLE SETS INCLUDE

Everyday Objects, Basic Verbs

USE ALSO FOR

Expression

Speechmark

(47) Picture story

AIM   *To wait, and then take a turn*

CARDS TO USE

Use cards showing single objects.

ACTIVITY

- Give every student a card and make sure they know the name of their object.
- Explain that you are going to tell a story and when they hear their object mentioned they must hold the card up in front of them.
- Make up a story, making sure you name the objects in random order.

SUITABLE SETS INCLUDE

Shape & Size, Animals & Birds, Transport & Vehicles

TIP

To make the activity harder, give every student two pictures.

USE ALSO FOR

Listening

(48) Match it

AIM   *To take turns in a group activity*

CARDS TO USE

Use small cards showing single objects.
You will need two of each card.
Choose about twenty pairs of cards.

ACTIVITY

- Arrange one set of cards face up on the table.
- Put the second set into a stack.
- Tell the students that they are going to match the pictures in the stack to the pictures on the table.
- Give the stack of cards to a student. Ask him to take the top picture, turn it over and put it on the matching card on the table.
- When he has finished, ask him to pass the stack to the next student.
- Then ask the second student to match two cards in the same way.
- Continue until all the cards have been paired up.

SUITABLE SETS INCLUDE

Categories and *More Categories* as there are two of each card in the packs.
Two packs of *Early Objects,* or *Early Actions* also work well.
If you adapt the activity slightly to matching cards that go together, you can use single packs of *Heads & Tails,* or *Early Opposites.*

TIP

For younger students, put the stack of cards face-up in a small box so that it is easy to pass round.

USE ALSO FOR

Attention

(49) Naming quiz

AIM   *To take turns in a team activity*

CARDS TO USE

Use cards showing objects, or use cards showing actions.
Choose about twenty pictures using vocabulary that the students may not know well.

ACTIVITY

- Split the students into two teams.
- Show a picture to the first team and ask them to name it. If they are right, give them a point.
- Do the same for the second team.
- Continue until you have used all the pictures, and see which team has more points.

SUITABLE SETS INCLUDE

Occupations, Leisure Time

TIP

The activity is harder if you ask one team member to name the picture.

USE ALSO FOR

Expression

(50) Listen and do

AIM   *To wait, and then take a turn*

CARDS TO USE

Use cards showing actions.
Choose actions that the students can easily mime.
Make a note of these verbs.

ACTIVITY

- Talk through the different actions with the students.
- Give everyone a card.
- Explain that you are going to tell them a story, and that when they hear the action on their card, they must do it. When it is another person's turn, they must just watch quietly.
- Make up a story, weaving the verbs into it, so that everyone has two or three turns.

SUITABLE SETS INCLUDE

Basic Verbs, Everyday Life

GOOD STORY THEMES INCLUDE

a party
a visit to the park
a playground
going to the shopping mall
on the beach
a walk in the country

USE ALSO FOR

Attention
Understanding

Speechmark

(51) Happy faces

AIM *To take turns in a game*

CARDS TO USE

Use small cards showing objects or actions.
Choose three cards for each student.
You will also need to make some small happy and sad faces from card. Put these into a bag.

ACTIVITY

- Show the happy and sad faces to the students. Explain that they will have three picture cards, and that they will take turns to put one of their cards on the table. Before they can put a picture down, they must pick a happy face from the bag. If they pick a sad face, they will miss a turn.
- Hand three picture cards to each student.
- Pass the bag of little faces to the first student. Ask him to take a face card from the bag. If it is happy, he can put one of his picture cards down. If it is sad, he must miss a turn, and pass the face bag to the next player straight away.
- The game ends when everyone has been able to put down all three cards.

SUITABLE SETS INCLUDE

Early Objects, Early Actions, Categories

(52) Songs and rhymes

AIM   *To wait, and then take a turn*

CARDS TO USE

Use cards showing single objects, or use cards showing simple actions.

Choose images that fit in with your song.

You will need to adapt a children's song for this activity.

ACTIVITY

- Seat the students in a circle and give each of them a picture.
- Tell them the name of the song, and the lines you will be singing.
- Sing the song together and ask them to stand up when their object or action is mentioned.

SUITABLE SETS INCLUDE

Animals & Birds, Early Actions, Basic Verbs

Examples of songs to sing

Old Macdonald – use animal pictures.

This is the way – use action pictures.

If you're happy and you know it – use action pictures.

We all clap hands together – use action pictures.

Speechmark P

53 Choose who's next

AIM   *To take turns to make a decision*

CARDS TO USE

Use cards showing a puzzle or anomaly.

ACTIVITY

- Give a small pack of the cards to a student.
- Ask him to look at the first card, and to tell the group the answer to the puzzle. 'The girl is ironing with a kettle.'
- Then ask him to choose who will have the next turn, and to hand him the pack of cards.
- Continue until each player has had two or three turns.

SUITABLE SETS INCLUDE

What's Wrong? What Is It? Fun Pictures

TIP

You may have to remind the students to include everyone in the game.

USE ALSO FOR

Life skills

Speechmark

Classification

This section covers word relationships and word meanings. It is concerned with similarities and differences of objects, actions and events. This is the basis of building categories and of concept formation. Using vocabulary in different contexts helps students to generalise their skills. Introducing new vocabulary helps them to develop richer language with a larger word-store.

These activities encourage understanding and logical thought. They will strengthen classification skills, and build up concept development. Students will increase their vocabulary, understand more about word meaning, and know when to use particular words.

You will find more activities that focus on categories and on concepts in other sections. Look in **Understanding** for activities on descriptions, functions and attributes of objects. Look in **Sequencing** for activities concerned with the concept of time. Look in **Life Skills** for activities involving feelings and emotions.

(54) Odd man out

AIM   *To recognise when one item is different from the rest of the group*

CARDS TO USE

Use cards showing single objects.
You will need six objects from a number of different categories.

ACTIVITY

- Show the students six cards, five from the same category and one that is quite different. You might choose five things from the kitchen, and one from the garden shed.
- Ask a student to find the odd man out.
- Continue with another group of cards for the next student.

SUITABLE SETS INCLUDE

Find the Link, Categories

TIP

For an easier activity, talk about the objects, leaving the odd one until last.

(55) Find another one

AIM   *To develop classification skills*

CARDS TO USE

Use cards showing objects.
You will need objects from several different categories.

ACTIVITY

- Show the students about five cards showing objects from the same category.
- Talk about what they are and why they belong to the same group.
- Add about five more cards. Some of these should have objects from the same category and some from different categories.
- Ask the students to find more objects in your chosen category.

SUITABLE SETS INCLUDE

Find the Link, Possessions and *Home*

TIP

If they manage this activity easily, ask them to think of other objects that could be included.

(56) Sort them out

AIM   *To develop classification skills according to a given criterion*

CARDS TO USE

Use cards showing objects.
You will need objects from several different categories.

ACTIVITY

- Show the students twelve pictures of objects from three different categories. You might choose food, clothes and toys.
- Tell them the names of the categories you have chosen.
- Ask them to sort the objects into their groups.

SUITABLE SETS INCLUDE

Find the Link, Categories

TIP

The activity is harder if the students have to sort the cards without knowing the category names.

You could ask them to sort objects by function such as 'things we cut with', 'things we write or colour with' and 'things we read'.

You could also ask them to sort objects by attribute such as 'things that are metal', 'things that are plastic' and 'things that are made of wood'.

Speechmark (5) P

(57) Opposite actions

AIM   *To understand opposite concepts*

CARDS TO USE

Use cards showing simple actions.

Choose verbs that have opposites.

ACTIVITY

- Show a card to the students.
- Ask a student to tell you what it shows. 'The boy is catching a ball.'
- Ask him for the opposite of 'catching'. 'Throwing.'
- Ask him to put 'throwing' into a sentence. 'The girl is throwing a stick for the dog.'
- Continue in turn round the group, choosing a new card each time.

Examples of word lists

(these pictures are from *Basic Verbs*)

catching	opening	dropping	washing
pulling	crying	drying	sleeping
throwing	closing	laughing	pushing

(these pictures are from *Familiar Verbs*)

buying	emptying	hiding	blowing
breaking	cleaning	climbing up	finishing
selling	filling	looking for	giving

USE ALSO FOR

Expression

58 More of the same

AIM *To add items to a category*

CARDS TO USE

Use cards showing scenes.
Choose topics that will interest your students.

ACTIVITY

- Show a card to the students.
- Talk together about what is on the card. 'It's a market. The woman is buying vegetables.'
- Ask the students to name what they can see in the picture. 'Cauliflower, oranges, bananas, potatoes, onions…'
- Then ask them to think of other fruit and vegetables that might have been there. 'Plums, cherries, strawberries, leeks…'

SUITABLE SETS INCLUDE

What's Missing? What's Inside? What's Different? Single cards from *Sequencing* sets

USE ALSO FOR

Expression

Speechmark **P**

(59) Decide for yourself

AIM   *To develop classification and decision-making skills*

CARDS TO USE

Use cards showing objects.
Choose objects that are unrelated.

ACTIVITY

- Show the students about twelve pictures.
- Ask a student to sort the cards into different groups. He can decide on the reasons for his grouping. He might choose *things inside the home* and *things outside the home*.
- Ask another student to group the cards in a different way. He might rearrange the objects into *things that are small, things that are medium sized* and *things that are large*.
- If any student thinks he can group in a third way, let him try.
- Continue with new cards for the next student.

SUITABLE SETS INCLUDE

More Categories, Possessions

USE ALSO FOR

Using language

(60) Shopping list

AIM   *To develop classification and decision-making skills*

CARDS TO USE

Use cards showing objects.
Choose objects that will fit in with your topic.

ACTIVITY

- Show the students about twenty cards.
- Tell them that they are going to make a shopping list.
- Ask them to choose pictures of things they will need for a particular purpose. You might choose *going on holiday*.

SUITABLE SETS INCLUDE

Possessions, Home

Other ideas are

preparing for a picnic	filling a bathroom cabinet
furnishing a bedroom	winter clothes
food for a party	going to school or university

TIP

To vary the activity, ask the students to choose gifts for different people.
These could include:

a teacher	a grandmother
a baby	a parent
a friend	someone they're visiting
a brother	a little girl

USE ALSO FOR

Life skills

(61) Happy families

AIM *To develop classification and decision-making skills*

CARDS TO USE

Use cards showing objects.

Choose a category for each student, and six cards for each category.

ACTIVITY

- Make sure the students know what the categories are, and tell each student which he is to collect.
- Shuffle the cards and deal four to each student.
- Spread the other cards face down on the table.
- The students take turns to pick up any card from the table. For each card they pick up, they must discard one.
- The winner is the first to get three (or four) cards in the same category.

SUITABLE SETS INCLUDE

Categories, Home

TIP

The activity works well with four students each collecting four cards. Six students should each collect three cards.

Adding two Joker cards that count for any other card will speed up the activity for students with shorter attention spans. Use pictures of people for Jokers.

USE ALSO FOR

Turn-taking

This page may be photocopied for instructional use only. *ColorCards Activities* © Vanessa Harrison 2006

(62) Same and different

Speechmark ColorCards Activities © Vanessa Harrison 2006 — This page may be photocopied for instructional use only.

AIM   *To recognise similarities and differences between objects*

CARDS TO USE

Use cards showing single objects.
Choose pairs of pictures that have similarities, such as a banana and a lemon, a pencil and a paintbrush.

ACTIVITY

- Put a pair of pictures on the table.
- Ask the students in what ways the two objects are the same.
- When they have listed all the similarities, ask them in what ways they are different.
- Continue with other pairs of pictures.

Examples of paired objects (these pictures are from *Everyday Objects*)
lamp and torch
jeans and shorts
mug and bowl
umbrella and coat
chips and bread
bed and chair

OTHER SUITABLE SETS INCLUDE

Categories, More Categories, Find the Link

USE ALSO FOR

Using language

(63) Think about it

AIM *To understand word relationships by linking nouns with verbs, or nouns with adjectives*

CARDS TO USE

Use cards showing simple objects.

Choose objects that can be associated with several verbs.

ACTIVITY

- Show the students one of the pictures.
- Name the object. 'An apple.'
- Ask the students to think of as many different things that it does as possible. This will encourage verbs. 'Eat, cut, cook, grow, chop, peel, slice, quarter…'
- Alternatively, ask them to think of words to describe it. This will encourage adjectives. 'Round, shiny, juicy, sweet, red, small…'
- Continue with other pictures.

Examples of suitable objects (these pictures are from *Find the Link*)

apple	potato
milk	car
dog	horse
book	water
knife	pencil
card	ball

USE ALSO FOR

Expression

(64) Can we do it?

AIM   *To understand word relationships by linking verbs with nouns*

CARDS TO USE

Use cards showing objects.

Choose pictures of objects that belong to three or four different categories.

ACTIVITY

- Put about twelve cards face up on the table.
- Look at the cards with the students and name the objects.
- Say a verb. 'Cut'.
- Ask a student to find an object that we can cut.
- Continue with other students until all they have chosen all the associated objects.
- Say another verb and continue the activity.

SUITABLE SETS INCLUDE

Home, Possessions, Find the Link

Example of word list (these pictures are from *Home*)

bowl	fork	colander
light bulb	clock	cup and saucer
knife	scissors	vegetable peeler
stool	sofa	dining chair
armchair	torch	desk lamp

Verbs to use with this group of objects

wash   break   cut   sit on   light

65 Connect

AIM *To recognise and explain relationships between objects*

CARDS TO USE

Use small cards showing single objects.
Choose a variety of objects from different categories.

ACTIVITY

- Put twenty to thirty cards face down on the table.
- Ask a student to turn over two of the cards and to name the pictures.
- Ask him if he can think of anything that links the two objects. This could be an attribute, a function, where they are found and so on.
- If his idea is convincing, he can keep that pair of cards.
- If he can't find a connection, he must return the cards to their original place on the table.
- Continue with the other students.
- You will need to add more cards as the activity proceeds. You are likely to have a few cards left at the end that will not connect.

SUITABLE SETS INCLUDE

Find the Link, More Categories

TIP

Be generous in accepting relationships especially if the student gives a good explanation.

USE ALSO FOR

Using language

Expression

Expression is the most distinctive aspect of language, socially and in the learning environment. Good verbal skills are fundamental to communicating well at home, at work and school and in more formal situations. This section deals with vocabulary and grammar. You should concentrate on accuracy before fluency throughout these activities.

When talking with your students, try to produce a relaxed environment with enough time to be unhurried. When they feel comfortable, they will want to respond, and also initiate language. Allow them enough time to think about what they have heard and to plan their own contribution.

Find a way to correct students' speech while remaining positive. Modelling the right response works well, as does expanding what they say. For immature students or those lacking confidence, give them alternative answers, so that they can respond by copying one of them.

The activities in this section will encourage the expression of single words, phrases, question forms and sentences. You'll find activities for building vocabulary, for developing different classes of words and for working on specific grammatical forms.

(66) Say the word

AIM *To practise emerging vocabulary*

CARDS TO USE

Use cards showing objects or cards showing actions.

ACTIVITY

- Show the students three pictures and name the objects or actions.
- Ask the students to name them too.
- Put the cards face down on the table.
- Point to a card and ask a student to name the hidden picture.
- Turn it over to check his answer.

SUITABLE SETS INCLUDE

Early Objects, Early Actions, Everyday Objects

TIP

Be prepared to give a clue or a hint to encourage success.

USE ALSO FOR

Attention

(67) That's wrong!

Speechmark © P This page may be photocopied for instructional use only *ColorCards Activities* © Vanessa Harrison 2006

AIM   *To practise using new vocabulary*

CARDS TO USE

Use cards showing objects.
Choose eight to ten cards.

ACTIVITY

- Show the students a picture and name it incorrectly.
- Ask a student to correct you.
- Continue with the rest of the pictures.
- If they are ready, let the students give wrong names to be corrected by the others.

SUITABLE SETS INCLUDE

Animals & Birds, Transport & Vehicles, Personal Items

TIP

You can use this activity for any part of speech as long as you emphasise the wrong word. 'The banana is *blue*. Is that the right colour?' 'He's *cutting* with his pen. Is that what he's doing?'

(68) Add on

AIM   *To increase vocabulary*

CARDS TO USE

Use cards showing objects or animals.
Choose about eight pictures.

ACTIVITY

- Put the cards face down on the table.
- Turn the first card over.
- The first student identifies the picture. 'It's a dog.'
- The next student adds something. 'It's a brown dog.'
- The next student adds something else. 'It's a brown dog, wagging its tail.'
- Continue round the group until the students run out of suitable additions.
- Start again with the next card.

SUITABLE SETS INCLUDE

Everyday Objects, Animals & Birds

TIP

Be prepared to help students by suggesting a new attribute such as size, weight or material.

USE ALSO FOR

Listening
Turn-taking

Speechmark

(69) Another word

AIM   *To increase vocabulary of different parts of speech*

CARDS TO USE

Use cards showing actions.

ACTIVITY

- Show a card to the students.
- Talk together about what it shows. 'The boy is grating cheese.'
- Ask a student to look at the picture again, and to tell you how he's grating the cheese. 'He's grating it carefully.'
- Ask another student to think of another way he could grate cheese. 'He could grate it quickly.'
- Continue with other pictures.

SUITABLE SETS INCLUDE

Basic Verbs, Familiar Verbs, Verb Tenses, Cause & Effect

TIP

As well as targeting adverbs, you could encourage different parts of speech by altering your approach. Using the same picture, for an adjective, you could ask, 'How do you think the boy feels?' For a preposition, 'Where is the cheese?' For a noun, 'What else could you grate?' For a verb, 'What else do we do with cheese?'

(70) Same again

AIM   *To increase verb vocabulary*

CARDS TO USE

Use pictures showing actions.
Choose about twelve verbs with vocabulary suitable for your group.

ACTIVITY

- Show one of the cards to the group.
- Ask a student to tell you what the picture shows. 'The girl is cooking sausages.'
- Ask him to think of another word to use for 'cooking'. 'Frying.'
- Ask the group to think of a third word. 'Sizzling.'
- Continue with other students and different pictures.

SUITABLE SETS INCLUDE

Basic Verbs (for an easier activity), *Familiar Verbs* (for a harder activity)

Example of word list (these pictures are from *Basic Verbs*)

build (make)	hug (cuddle)
carry (hold)	paint (decorate)
cook (fry)	run (jog)
cry (sob)	sleep (snooze)
drink (swallow)	talk (chat)
eat (munch)	watch (look at)

Example of word list (these pictures are from *Familiar Verbs*)

ask (enquire, request)	mix (combine, blend)
clean (wash, wipe)	pin (fasten, attach)
fill (load, pack)	put away (tidy, stack)
help (assist, aid)	stick (fix, place)
look for (uncover, locate)	stroke (caress, pet)
make (put together, create)	tie (do up, fasten)

(71) Yes and no

AIM   *To answer questions with 'yes' and 'no'*

CARDS TO USE

Use cards showing objects, or cards showing actions.
Choose pictures that will interest the students, and with the right level of difficulty.

ACTIVITY

- Tell the students that you are going to ask them some questions, and that they must answer with 'yes' or 'no'.
- Show them a picture and ask a student a suitable question. He must answer 'yes' or 'no'.
- Continue with other students and different pictures.

SUITABLE SETS INCLUDE

Everyday Objects, Familiar Verbs

TIP

For an easier activity, use pictures of objects, and ask questions about their attributes and uses. 'Is a bus made of wood?', 'Can you boil water in a kettle?' For a harder activity, use pictures of actions, and ask more complex questions. 'Can you make a cake without using flour?'

USE ALSO FOR

Understanding

(72) One, two and three

AIM   *To use adjectives*

CARDS TO USE

Use cards showing single objects.
Choose pictures of a variety of objects, with different attributes.

ACTIVITY

- Put a group of cards on the table.
- Pick up the first card and describe it using a single adjective, 'a blue bowl'.
- Ask the students one at a time to pick up a picture, and to describe it using one describing word. They could choose colour again, or choose a different attribute, 'a little flower'.
- Pick up another card, and describe the object using two adjectives, 'a big, shiny bike'.
- Ask the students to do the same with other pictures.
- Finally, pick up a card, and describe the object using three adjectives, 'a round, red, bouncy ball'.
- Ask the students to try to do the same.

SUITABLE SETS INCLUDE

Everyday Objects, Categories

TIP

Be ready to help by suggesting suitable attributes to anyone having difficulties.

(73) Simon says

AIM *To use verb phrases*

CARDS TO USE

Use cards showing simple actions.

Choose verbs that have an object.

ACTIVITY

- Play a variation of this traditional game using cards.
- Put six to eight cards face down on the table.
- Each student takes a turn at being Simon.
- Simon turns over a card and tells the others to mime the action on the card.
- If Simon uses the words 'Simon says', the students must mime the action.
- If Simon just gives a command, the students must ignore it.
- For example, if Simon says 'Simon says eat a banana', the others must mime eating a banana. If Simon says 'throw a ball', any student that joins in is out for the rest of the round.
- Continue with the next student turning over a card to give his instruction.

SUITABLE SETS INCLUDE

Basic Verbs, Everyday Life

USE ALSO FOR

Listening

Speechmark

74 Owners

AIM   *To use possessives, or to use pronouns*

CARDS TO USE

Use cards showing people and objects on the same card.

ACTIVITY

For possessives

- Show a card to the students, and talk about it together. 'The boy is driving the car. It's the boy's car.'
- Give one or two cards to each student.
- In turn, ask them to describe their objects in the same way. 'The girl's drink.' 'The man's pen.'

For pronouns

- Talk about the pronouns 'he', 'she' and 'they', and when to use them.
- Look at the cards one at a time, and ask the students to say a sentence beginning with a pronoun. 'She is drinking.' 'He is writing.' 'They are looking at the map.'

SUITABLE SETS INCLUDE

Problem Solving, Adjectives, Prepositions

USE ALSO FOR

Turn-taking

(75) Today, yesterday and tomorrow

AIM   *To use different verb tenses*

CARDS TO USE

Use cards showing actions.
Choose verbs that have an object.

ACTIVITY

- Talk to the students about how verbs change depending on whether we are talking about the present, the past or the future.
- Choose three students and seat them in a row.
- Show them a picture.
- Call one student 'Today', the next 'Yesterday' and the third 'Tomorrow'. (For more advanced students, use the words 'Present', 'Past' and 'Future'.)
- Ask each in turn to describe what is happening in the picture using the right verb tense.
- The first student must start with the word 'today', the next with the word 'yesterday' and the third with the word 'tomorrow'.
- If all goes to plan, the students will say in sequence something like the following:

'Today, the girl is feeding her rabbit.'
'Yesterday, the girl fed her rabbit.'
'Tomorrow, the girl will feed her rabbit.'

SUITABLE SETS INCLUDE

Basic Verbs, Familiar Verbs, Cause & Effect

Speechmark

(76) Where?

This page may be photocopied for instructional use only. *ColorCards Activities* © Vanessa Harrison 2006

AIM   *To ask and answer questions using the word 'where'*

CARDS TO USE

Use cards showing groups of objects.

Choose about ten pictures.

ACTIVITY

- Show a picture to the students.
- Choose an object in the picture, and ask a student where it is. 'Where is the doll?'
- He must reply with a phrase such as 'on the shelf' or 'next to the teddy'.
- Ask the students, in turn, to take a card, and to ask a 'where' question to their neighbour.

SUITABLE SETS INCLUDE

What's Inside? What's Different?

USE ALSO FOR

Understanding

(77) Who?

AIM   *To ask and answer questions, using the word 'who'*

CARDS TO USE

Use cards showing scenes with people.
Choose about ten pictures.

ACTIVITY

- Show a picture to the students.
- Choose a subject, and ask a student who is doing an action. 'Who is cleaning the windows?'
- He must reply with the name of the person. 'The man.'
- Ask the students, in turn, to take a card, and to ask a 'who' question to their neighbour.

SUITABLE SETS INCLUDE

Individual pictures from any *Sequencing* set, *Personal Safety, Emotions, Personal Relationships.*

TIP

Choose some cards that have more than one person doing the same activity.
This will allow the students to practise the word 'who' with plural verbs.

USE ALSO FOR

Understanding

(78) Why?

AIM *To ask questions using 'why', and to answer using 'because'*

CARDS TO USE

Use cards showing actions or cards showing scenes with people.

ACTIVITY

- Show a card to the students.
- Ask a suitable question. 'Why is the boy happy?' or 'Why is the family arguing?'
- Ask a student to answer starting with 'because'.
- Give a card to another student.
- Ask him to look at what is happening, and then ask his neighbour a 'why' question.
- Continue round the group.

SUITABLE SETS INCLUDE

Any *Verb* set, single cards from any *Sequencing* set

USE ALSO FOR

Listening
Understanding

(79) Twenty questions

AIM *To use simple question forms*

CARDS TO USE

Use cards showing single objects.

ACTIVITY

- Tell the students that they are going to guess what objects are on hidden cards. Talk about the sort of information that could be useful to know. Suggest that they ask questions about the size of the object, its shape, where it's found, what it's made of, whether it's useful and so on.
- Put the cards face down on the table.
- Ask a student to pick up a card, to look at it, but not to let the others see it.
- Ask him the first question to discover what the object is. 'Would it fit into a shopping bag?'
- Ask the students to ask questions in turn to learn more.
- See if they can guess the object in less than twenty questions.
- Repeat with other students and different cards.

SUITABLE SETS INCLUDE

Everyday Objects, Home, Possessions

USE ALSO FOR

Turn-taking

Speechmark

80 Making sentences

AIM *To use sentences*

CARDS TO USE

Use cards showing people, and cards showing possessions.
Choose a sentence structure for your activity.

ACTIVITY

- Give everyone a picture of a person.
- Put a group of pictures of objects on the table. You will need enough pictures to let everyone have a good choice.
- Using a picture of a person and a picture of an object, say a sentence such as 'The boy has a skateboard.'
- Ask each student to choose an object that his person might like to have.
- Ask them, in turn, to say a similar sentence using both of their cards.

SUITABLE SETS INCLUDE

For people – *Basic Verbs, Occupations*
For objects – *Everyday Objects, Possessions*

TIP

You can use other sentence structures in this activity. Choose a structure for your teaching or therapy aim. You might model 'This boy would like a skateboard' or 'The boy is going to buy a new skateboard'.

Using Language

Once students' expressive language is sufficiently developed, they need to learn to adapt it to fit in with different circumstances. The content of their language and their style should vary with the situation and with the people present. There are times when spontaneous and informal speech has to be adjusted to suit a particular situation. You should encourage fluency throughout these activities, as well as suitable vocabulary and accurate expression.

This section deals with the many different functions of language. You will find activities that focus on asking for needs, making statements, describing and explaining. Other activities help story telling, logical thought, imaginative thinking and problem solving. Your students will be able to practise making observations, and describing events and experiences. They will also explore, develop and clarify their ideas. As a group, they will be able to discuss possibilities and give reasons for their opinions.

There are more activities for using language in different contexts in the **Life Skills** section.

(81) Shopping

AIM *To ask for items clearly and precisely*

CARDS TO USE

Use cards showing food.

Choose pictures of basic food items for shopping (or choose pictures of prepared dishes for a restaurant or take-away activity).

ACTIVITY

- Put a selection of cards face up on the table.
- Ask one of the students to be the shopkeeper.
- Ask the other students, in turn, to come to the shop and to ask for two items.
- Encourage them to use accurate language rather than relying on pointing or using non-specific words.
- Help the shopkeeper to ask questions about their purchases such as 'How many would you like?' or 'Do you need a bag?'

SUITABLE SETS INCLUDE

Food, Snack Time, Categories

82 Describing pictures

AIM   *To describe scenes and events*

CARDS TO USE

Use cards showing scenes with people.

ACTIVITY

- Show a picture to the group and describe it using two or three simple sentences. 'The family is having a picnic. It is a sunny day. They are just starting their lunch.'
- Give a different card to a student and ask him to describe the scene.
- Continue with the other students and new scenes.
- Help them to think of all aspects of their scenes such as the situation, the people present and the activity.

SUITABLE SETS INCLUDE

What's Missing? What's Wrong? Individual cards from *Sequencing* sets, *Personal Relationships*

TIP

After all the students have had a turn, try asking them to describe a scene without the rest of the group seeing the card. Then ask them to show the card, so that the group can say whether they were able to imagine the scene well, or what other information would have been useful.

(83) How do you do it?

AIM   *To explain how to do an activity*

CARDS TO USE

Use one of the *Sequencing* sets.
Choose sequences showing everyday activities.

ACTIVITY

- Order the cards of one sequence.
- Talk through the cards one at a time, using them to explain how to perform the activity. 'Notice that the bin is full. Take the bag of rubbish away. Put a fresh bag into the bin.'
- Ask one of the students to talk through the same sequence.
- Then ask the students to describe the activities in different sequences.
- Be ready to help them to order their sequences, and to explain the activity on each card briefly and accurately.
- Continue until everyone in the group has had a turn.

SUITABLE SETS INCLUDE

Basic Sequences, Simple Sequences, Early Sequences

TIP

For a harder activity, give them just one card from a sequence.

USE ALSO FOR

Sequencing

(84) Picture differences

AIM   *To explain the differences between two similar pictures*

CARDS TO USE

Use pairs of cards that show the same scene or activity, but with changes.

What's Different? has pairs of cards showing differences.

What's Missing? has pairs of cards showing missing objects.

What's Inside? has pairs of cards showing storage places and their contents.

ACTIVITY

- Show a pair of cards to the students.
- Explain to them in what ways the two cards are different. Use accurate language to give a detailed explanation.
- Ask a student to do the same with another pair of pictures.
- Continue with the other students.
- Repeat the activity, but this time, ask the students to keep their pictures hidden as they explain their differences.
- When they have finished, ask them to show their pictures to the others.
- Then talk together about how well they described the two pictures.

85) A new ending

AIM   *To develop logical thought*

CARDS TO USE

Use a *Sequencing* set.
Choose whole sequences that tell stories.

ACTIVITY

- Help the students to sequence one of the stories.
- Talk through the story with them.
- Remove the final card and suggest a different ending to the story.
- Ask the students to think of other endings.
- Encourage them to use their imagination to think of unlikely endings as well as the more obvious.

SUITABLE SETS INCLUDE

Sequences: 6 & 8-Step for Children, Sequences: 6 & 8-Step for Adults

USE ALSO FOR

Sequencing

86 Storylines

AIM   *To develop story telling*

CARDS TO USE

Use sequences from any of the *Sequencing* sets.
Choose sequences that tell a story.

ACTIVITY

- Put one of the sequences on the table with the cards in the right order.
- Tell the story, card by card, emphasising the beginning, the middle and the end.
- Ask one of the students to retell the story.
- Repeat with the other students, changing to a new story after two or three turns.
- When all students have had a turn, use the same sequences to ask them about parts of the stories. 'What happened after the boy bought the ice cream?' 'What happened before the children washed the car?' 'The boy chose a fish. What happened next?'

SUITABLE SETS INCLUDE

Sequences 4-Step, Sequences 6 & 8-Step for Children, Sequences 6 & 8-Step for Adults

USE ALSO FOR

Sequencing

Speechmark ⑤ P

(87) Charades

AIM   *To ask questions in a team game*

CARDS TO USE

Use cards showing actions.
Choose vocabulary that will challenge your students slightly. You will need at least one picture for each student.
You will also need two large envelopes.

ACTIVITY

- Divide the group in half.
- Move them to different sides of the room.
- Give each team an envelope containing half the pictures.
- Explain that in turn, they must take a picture from their envelope, and mime the action it shows to their own team.
- Team members can ask questions to help them guess the action, but the actor must only answer 'yes' and 'no'.
- As soon as a team guesses an action correctly, the next member takes an action picture from the envelope and mimes that activity.
- The team that finishes their cards first is the winner.

SUITABLE SETS INCLUDE

Basic Verbs, Familiar Verbs, individual cards from *Cause & Effect* or *Problem Solving*

USE ALSO FOR

Turn-taking

(88) Work it out

AIM   *To develop logical thought*

CARDS TO USE

Use any two-step sequences.
Choose sequences in which the second part follows straight on from the first part.

ACTIVITY

- Show the second part of a sequence to the students.
- Talk through the activity. 'The boy is pulling a face because his dinner tastes horrible.'
- Ask a student to tell you what he thinks might have happened just before. Encourage him to look for a clue in the picture. (There are salt and pepper mills on the table.)
- Ask other students for their ideas.
- Show the first card of the sequence to see what did happen.
- Continue with other students and different sequences.

SUITABLE SETS INCLUDE

Simple Sequences, Cause & Effect, Problem Solving, Guess What?

TIP

For a harder activity, use sequences with a time lag between the actions shown on the two cards.

(89) Desert Island

AIM
To encourage imaginative thought

CARDS TO USE
Use cards showing single objects.
Choose objects that interest your students.

ACTIVITY

- Put the pictures face up on the table. Make sure that there is a good selection.
- Ask the students to pick up a picture of an object that they would like to have with them if they were going to live on a desert island. It can be something useful, or something that they just enjoy.
- Ask them, in turn, to explain why they chose their object, and how they would use it on the island.
- Talk with them about other aspects of desert island living, such as what they would eat, who they would miss, and how they could spend their time.

SUITABLE SETS INCLUDE
Possessions, More Categories

TIP
Extend this activity by choosing other destinations such as the South Pole or the Moon.

USE ALSO FOR
Turn-taking

(90) Sound stories

AIM   *To take part in cooperative story telling*

CARDS TO USE

Use cards showing objects and the CD from one of the *Listening* sets. Choose a variety of objects, and perhaps some animals.

ACTIVITY

- Play five or six sounds from the CD.
- Make sure the students can identify them and match them to their pictures.
- Divide the students into groups of two or three.
- Leave the matching pictures in view, and ask them to make up a story linking some of the sounds.
- Ask a member of each small group to tell their story.
- As they do so, replay the sounds in the right places. They will enjoy hearing them again.
- See how the stories compare.

TIP

The activity is easier to do (and to organise) if you just use picture cards.

Using sounds as well does make it more fun.

Speechmark

91 Help

AIM   *To develop problem solving*

CARDS TO USE

Use cards showing simple activity.

ACTIVITY

- Show a card to the students. Talk together about what is happening. 'The boy is kicking a football.'
- Make up a problem based on the picture. 'He kicks the ball into the road', or 'The ball breaks a window'. Ask a student to suggest what the boy could do next.
- Ask the rest of the group for different suggestions.
- Continue with other students and different cards.

SUITABLE SETS INCLUDE

Basic Verbs, Familiar Verbs, Simple Sequences, Basic Sequences

TIP

For an easier activity, use pictures of objects, and ask questions such as where to buy it, how to keep it safe, or how it works.

USE ALSO FOR

Listening
Life skills

(92) Just a minute

AIM *To talk on a subject for a given length of time*

CARDS TO USE

Use cards showing scenes.
You will also need a watch with a second hand.

ACTIVITY

- Put a selection of cards face up on the table.
- Decide on a length of time, and explain to the students that they are going to try to talk to the group for that amount of time, using one of the scenes.
- Ask a confident student to choose a card that he likes.
- Let him look at it, and then talk to the others about it from any point of view.
- Time him from when he starts, and let him know when he can stop.
- Continue with other students and different cards.

SUITABLE SETS INCLUDE

Social Behaviour, Personal Safety, Emotions, single cards from *Sequencing* sets

TIP

For some students, twenty seconds will be long enough. Others may be able to manage a full minute.

Speechmark P

93 Discussion

AIM   *To take part in a discussion*

CARDS TO USE

Use pictures showing activity.

Choose scenes with more than one topic or theme.

Tell the students that you are going to show them some pictures where people are busy. You will ask them a question to do with what is happening. They can then answer, one at a time. Remind them to listen to other people's ideas carefully and quietly.

Explain that it is not always easy to know when to talk and when to listen. In a group, they will have to listen more than talk!

ACTIVITY

- Show a picture to the students.
- Introduce the theme. 'The boy is crossing a busy road with a buggy and a dog.'
- Ask a question to promote discussion. 'Can you think of a safer way he could cross the road?'
- If the discussion is going well, widen it to include other aspects of the situation; road safety in this case.

SUITABLE SETS INCLUDE

Personal Safety, Social Behaviour, Sequences 6 & 8-Step for Children, Sequences 6 & 8-Step for Adults

TIP

Start off with three or four students taking part only.

USE ALSO FOR

Listening

Turn-taking

Life Skills

Students with well-developed language and good presentation skills are well on the way to becoming effective communicators. Social skills are important too to enable them to be responsive, and to adapt to different people in a variety of situations.

They also need to learn how to manage their own feelings, to recognise the feelings of other people, and to be able to react in an appropriate way. Students who feel good about themselves and are open to the needs of others, are likely to be popular in their group. They are also in a strong position to enjoy, and to benefit from, the learning environment.

The activities in this section are concerned with self-awareness, an appreciation of the differences and needs of others, speaking styles, aspects of non-verbal communication, feelings and emotions and the language used to express them, and aspects of caring and responsibility.

(94) Feelings

AIM *To practise using words to describe feelings*

CARDS TO USE

Use cards that show single people with expressive faces.
You will also need some cards showing scenes with people.

ACTIVITY

- Show the pictures to the students, and talk about them together. Explain to the students that how people look can tell us about how they are feeling. Encourage them to use as many 'feeling' words as they can.
- Then show them some cards of scenes with people.
- Ask them to look for people showing the feelings that you have talked about together.

SUITABLE SETS INCLUDE

For individual people – *Emotions, How's Teddy? Cause & Effect, Expressive Verbs*

For scenes – *Emotions, Sequences 4-Step, Sequences: 6 & 8-Step for Children, Sequences: 6 & 8-Step for Adults*

TIP

Choose feelings that are easier to understand, such as 'happy', 'sad', 'tired' and 'excited' to start with.

USE ALSO FOR

Expression
Using language

(95) Do we like it?

AIM   *To recognise that people have different preferences*

CARDS TO USE

Use cards showing food or animals.

ACTIVITY

- Tell the students that they are going to talk to the group in turn. The others should listen carefully.
- Show a card to the students.
- Ask them to say why they like, or why they don't like the object on the card.
- When they have all had a turn, show them a second card.
- Now ask them to say why they like or don't like the new object.
- Repeat the activity once or twice more.
- When they have finished, talk together about how different people have different likes and dislikes.

SUITABLE SETS INCLUDE

Food, Snack Time, Animals & Birds, Find The Link

USE ALSO FOR

Using language

Speechmark (S) P

96 Choosing a present

AIM   *To make choices knowing other people's preferences*

CARDS TO USE

Use cards showing objects that could be suitable for gifts.

ACTIVITY

- Tell the students that you have chosen some presents for different people, and that you are not sure whether they will like them.
- Say the name of a person, and then show them one of the cards.
- Ask a student whether they think that the person will like this present. If they answer is 'no', ask them to suggest something that they might like.
- Continue until everyone has had at least one turn.

Example of word list for People

teacher	aunt
baby	mother
teenager	someone in hospital
little girl	someone moving to a new house
grandmother	gardener
cook	friend

TIP

The students will enjoy the inclusion of one or two unsuitable items that few people would want.

SUITABLE SETS INCLUDE

Categories, Possessions

(97) Body talk

AIM *To explore some aspects of body language*

CARDS TO USE

Use cards showing two or more people.

Choose pictures where people are touching each other, or are very close.

ACTIVITY

- Introduce the idea of body language to the students.
- Talk in more detail about:

    facial expression, and how it can reveal feelings

    eye contact, and how it can help communication

    touch, and when it feels comfortable and appropriate

    personal space, and the need for privacy.

- Show the cards to the students one at a time, and look together at the body language of the people shown.
- Encourage the students to think of situations where awareness of body language might help them and the people they're with.

SUITABLE SETS INCLUDE

Emotions, Sequences 4-Step, Expressive Verbs, Personal Relationships

USE ALSO FOR

Using language

Speechmark (S) P

98) How do I sound?

This page may be photocopied for instructional use only. *ColorCards Activities* © Vanessa Harrison 2006

AIM *To understand that voices can show feelings*

CARDS TO USE

Use cards with individual people showing feelings or emotions.
You will also need a list of phrases.

ACTIVITY

* Show the pictures to the students, and talk together about how the people are feeling.
* Explain that when people talk, their feelings can influence how they sound.
* Choose a sentence such as 'I've got something to tell you', and say it in a voice to match one of the emotions on the cards.
* Ask a student to find the card showing the right person.
* Use the same phrase in a different voice to match one of the other pictures.
* Continue with other voices, and then other phrases.

SUITABLE SETS INCLUDE

Emotions, How's Teddy? Expressive Verbs

Examples of phrases to use

'I'm going out.'
'The letter came this morning.'
'They're getting married next week.'
'I slept for three hours.'
'In the end, the Red team won the match.'
'I don't know where my purse is.'
'Your skirt is very short.'
'The train arrived at half past seven.'

TIP

Choose very distinctive feelings such as 'happy', 'sad', 'tired' and 'cross' to start with.

To make the activity harder, ask the students to try using different voices.

(99) How do they feel?

AIM   *To develop awareness of other people's feelings*

CARDS TO USE
Use cards showing scenes with people.

ACTIVITY

- Show a card to the students and talk together about what is happening.
- Ask them about how they think someone in the scene might be feeling. 'The woman feels upset because the bathroom's in a mess.'
- Talk with them about how one person's behaviour can affect how someone else feels. 'The boy didn't clear up in the bathroom. That's why she's upset.'
- Continue with other cards.

SUITABLE SETS INCLUDE
For people showing some emotion, cards from the longer *Sequencing* sets

For people showing strong emotions, cards from *Emotions* and *Social Behaviour*

USE ALSO FOR
Using language

(100) Taking care

AIM   *To develop an awareness of caring*

CARDS TO USE
Use cards showing responsible or caring behaviour.
Choose scenes that the students could experience.
Choose a wide age range of caring people.

ACTIVITY
- Show a picture to the students.
- Ask a student to find the person being helpful. 'The lady next door.'
- Ask another student to explain in what way she is being helpful. 'She is letting the children get their ball back.'
- Continue with other pictures until all the students have had a turn at finding a helpful person, and at giving an explanation.

SUITABLE SETS INCLUDE
Social Behaviour, Sequences: 6 & 8-Step for Children, Sequences: 6 & 8-Step for Adults, Emotions, Personal Relationships

USE ALSO FOR
Using language

101 Helping

AIM *To develop awareness of responsibility*

CARDS TO USE

Use cards showing one busy person.
Choose a variety of ages, and of activities.

ACTIVITY

- Talk to the students about being helpful. Talk about the difference between helping when someone asks us to help, and offering to help when someone looks busy, or perhaps tired.
- Show them one of the cards. Talk together about what the person is doing. 'The woman is cleaning the floor after a party.'
- Ask a student how he thinks he could help that person. 'I could clear the table for her.'
- Ask the others whether they agree.
- Continue with the other cards until all the students have had at least one turn at answering.

SUITABLE SETS INCLUDE

Basic Verbs, Familiar Verbs, Problem Solving

TIP

Include one or two cards in which the best way to help could be to leave the person alone!

USE ALSO FOR

Using language

Speechmark P

Index

Activity name	Number	Skill area	Page
Same and different	62	Classification	87
Say it again	31	Auditory memory	47
Say the word	66	Expression	93
Sequencing activities	39	Sequencing	58
Shopping	81	Using language	111
Shopping list	60	Classification	85
Simon says	73	Expression	100
Songs and rhymes	52	Turn-taking	74
Sort them out	56	Classification	81
Sound link	16	Listening	25
Sound sequencing	11	Listening	20
Sound stories	90	Using language	120
Sounds around	10	Listening	19
Spot the mistake	40	Sequencing	59
Storylines	86	Using language	116
Taking care	100	Life skills	134
That's wrong!	67	Expression	94
The right place	41	Sequencing	60
Think about it	63	Classification	88
Think again	29	Understanding	40
This and that	32	Auditory memory	48
Today, yesterday and tomorrow	75	Expression	102
Twenty questions	79	Expression	106
What else?	13	Listening	22
What's it for?	20	Understanding	31
What's it like?	21	Understanding	32
What's that sound?	9	Listening	17
Where it is	22	Understanding	33
Where?	76	Expression	103
Who?	77	Expression	104
Who can it be?	30	Understanding	42
Why?	78	Expression	105
Work it out	88	Using language	118
Yes and no	71	Expression	98

Activities for each skill area

Skill area	Main activities	Other useful activities
Attention	1–8	13 15 16 32 35 36 48 50 66
Listening	9–17	8 31 37 47 68 73 78 91 93
Understanding	18–30	6 7 8 34 35 50 71 76 77 78
Auditory memory	31–37	7 9 10 11 12 13 14 23 44
Sequencing	38–44	2 31 45 83 85 86
Turn-taking	45–53	36 42 43 61 68 74 79 87 89 93
Classification	54–65	6 20 21 23 25 26 33
Expression	66–80	33 46 49 57 58 63 94
Using language	81–93	43 59 62 65 94 95 97 99 100 101
Life skills	94–101	25 27 42 53 60 91

List of ColorCards

All the sets include instructions, either in a booklet or on a card (Pocket ColorCards and Pocket ColorCards for Adults).

FIND THE LINK

A word finding and category game. 200 hexagonal cards and a game board.

Pocket ColorCards

Pocket-sized sets of flashcards, designed to support teaching and therapy in the clinic, school and home.

EARLY ACTIONS

An imaginative way to develop verb vocabulary.

EARLY OBJECTS

Develops a naming vocabulary through play.

EARLY OPPOSITES

Introduces opposites in an entertaining way.

EARLY SEQUENCES

An engaging introduction to sequencing.

FUN PICTURES

Simple images with a deliberate mistake in every card.

GUESS WHAT?

2-step sequences to give an introduction to predicting outcomes.

HEADS & TAILS

An exciting matching game.

HOW MANY?

An enjoyable introduction to number.

HOW'S TEDDY?
Introduces feelings in a simple and lively way.

MATCH UP
A creative matching game using objects in different forms and contexts.

SHAPE & SIZE
Shape and size illustrated in an appealing way.

SNACK TIME
A versatile set to broaden food vocabulary.

Pocket ColorCards for Adults

Compact, photographic flashcards to support communication of older adults in hospital, at home or in the clinic.

EVERYDAY LIFE
A comprehensive series of daily living activities.

IN HOSPITAL
An essential pack for staff and visitors.

LEISURE TIME
Encourages discussion of activities and interests.

PERSONAL ITEMS
A versatile set illustrating personal belongings.

Sequencing ColorCards

Sets of sequencing cards varying from 2-step to 8-step sequences. Some show familiar activities and some are in story form.

BASIC SEQUENCES
3-step sequences of familiar activities.

CAUSE & EFFECT
2-step sequences to develop logical thinking skills.

PROBLEM SOLVING
2-step sequences showing everyday problems, and alternative ways to solve them.

SEQUENCES: 4-STEP
Twelve lively 4-step sequences featuring familiar activities.

SEQUENCES: 6 & 8-STEP FOR ADULTS
6 and 8-step sequences with a variety of stories. Provides excellent opportunities for language work.

SEQUENCES: 6 & 8-STEP FOR CHILDREN
A more complex set including both 6 and 8-step sequences with a variety of stories. An excellent resource for language work.

SEQUENCES: VERB TENSES
3-step sequences to illustrate past, present and future verb tenses.

SIMPLE SEQUENCES
2 and 3-step sequences of home-based activities.

Verb series

A comprehensive series of Verb sets to teach vocabulary, sentence structure and grammatical forms.

ADJECTIVES

Shows paired adjectives in context, with several examples of each.

BASIC VERBS

Clear images of the most frequently used and easily recognisable verbs.

EMOTIONS

Pictures of real people in a range of situations. Designed to promote an awareness of feelings.

EVERYDAY OBJECTS

Domestic objects arranged in six colour-coded categories.

EXPRESSIVE VERBS

Simple actions that have intrinsic meaning. Illustrate how we use our bodies to enhance communication.

FAMILIAR VERBS

Further frequently used verbs. Associated objects are included to give an idea of place.

OBJECTS & OWNERS

A variety of people to match with their possessions. For developing concepts and word relationships.

ODD ONE OUT

Cards of graded difficulty to develop categorisation skills.

PREPOSITIONS

Illustrates the main prepositions essential to the teaching of basic language skills.

VERB TENSES

A colourful strip book to teach past, present and future tenses, displayed in threes.

WHAT'S ADDED?

One card of each pair shows a complete scene, and the other shows the scene with up to three additional objects that shouldn't be there.

WHAT'S DIFFERENT?

There are three differences between each pair of cards in this set. The task is to identify and explain the differences.

WHAT'S INSIDE?

Pairs of cards show storage places or containers, and the various objects found inside them.

WHAT IS IT?

Objects in this set are either shown from an unusual angle, or only shown in part.

WHAT'S MISSING?

One card of each pair shows a complete scene, and another shows the scene with five items missing.

WHAT'S WRONG?

Each humorous card shows an absurdity to encourage expressive language.

ColorCards Display Stand

Holds ColorCards vertically. Available in packs of four or eight. Use them singly, or clip one or more packs together. They are particularly helpful for students with attention difficulties or visual problems.

ColorLibrary

ColorLibrary sets are file boxes of 96 cards. Divided into six categories, they provide a rich resource of essential vocabulary.

ANIMALS & BIRDS

Features a selection of living creatures from all over the world. Divided into six categories: wild land animals, domestic animals, insects and mini-beasts, reptiles and amphibians, marine life and birds.

FOOD

Contains six categories: fruit, vegetables, basics, prepared food, drinks and snacks.

HOME

Contains items from six rooms of a home: lounge, diner, kitchen, bedroom, bathroom and study.

OCCUPATIONS

Photographed on location, these cards feature arts and crafts, trades, public services, health workers, transport, and general occupations.

POSSESSIONS

A variety of everyday items categorised into care, children, domestic, leisure, personal and toiletries.

SPORT & LEISURE

A popular choice for everyone, the categories include adventure sports, team sports, individual sports, hobbies, pastimes and entertainment.

TRANSPORT & VEHICLES

This transportation set features the following categories: air, water, rail, personal, cycles, and service/works vehicles.

Listening Skills

With the sounds on CDs, these sound and picture matching activities are easy to use. Ideal for working with groups or individuals.
Each set contains 40 cards and one CD.

INDOOR SOUNDS

Arranged in four groups of ten, this set includes forty familiar indoor sounds.

OUTDOOR SOUNDS

Arranged in four groups of ten, this set includes forty sounds heard outside.

SEQUENCING SOUNDS

Contains the individual sounds of fourteen two-step sequences and four three-step sequences, providing forty sounds in total.

Multi-Match

MULTI-MATCH CATEGORIES

24 Categories each of four cards provide a versatile resource of 96 different cards for language-based activities. Each card appears twice to extend the use of this set. The images are suitable for the whole age range.

MULTI-MATCH MORE CATEGORIES

With the same format as Multi-Match Categories, this set features Colours, Patterns and Shapes.

LOTTO CLIP FRAMES

For making customised lotto activities from Multi-Match sets. 8 per pack

Illustrated ColorCards, Skills for Daily Living

PERSONAL RELATIONSHIPS

Shows different kinds of relationships, and also the progression of attachments from initial meeting to sexual activity.

PERSONAL SAFETY

Promotes understanding and discussion of health and safety issues.

SOCIAL BEHAVIOUR

Illustrated cards to teach awareness of sociable behaviour. This set includes examples of both good and poor awareness of social skills.